BEXLEY
BUSES

VERNON SMITH

AMBERLEY

First published 2019

Amberley Publishing
The Hill, Stroud
Gloucestershire, GL5 4EP

www.amberley-books.com

Copyright © Vernon Smith, 2019

The right of Vernon Smith to be identified as
the Author of this work has been asserted in
accordance with the Copyright, Designs and
Patents Act 1988.

ISBN 978 1 4456 7676 0 (print)
ISBN 978 1 4456 7677 7 (ebook)

British Library Cataloguing in Publication Data.
A catalogue record for this book is available from
the British Library.

Typesetting by Amberley Publishing.
Printed in the UK.

Introduction

The period from 1983 until 1993 was one of the more interesting times in the ever-changing history of buses in South East London. Until now, despite the usual tinkering with routes, and the routine replacement of vehicles, there was an air of stability, but by the early part of the 1980s all that would have changed.

Bexleyheath garage was originally built in 1935 as a trolleybus depot, converting to motor bus operation in 1959. By the early 1980s, the garage's allocation of unreliable DMS buses were being replaced with new Leyland Titans. The garage had a large forecourt, which also served as a terminus for routes 122 and 160, and a large rear area that was often used to store out-of-service or new vehicles. Nearby were the new Plumstead garage, and also Sidcup garage, which had recently been rebuilt. Both garages also had allocations of Titans and Routemasters, while Sidcup had a small allocation of Metrobuses (allocated there as part of a comparative trial between the Metrobus, Titan and DMS classes) and Plumstead had the remnants of the MD class Metropolitans. On the edge of London was London Country's Dartford garage, whose routes penetrated London as far as Thamesmead, Belvedere and Erith using standard NBC vehicles, such as Atlanteans and Leyland Nationals.

The deregulation of buses in 1986 excluded London, but London Regional Transport did start putting individual routes out to tender, with the first route, the 81, being won by London Buslines, who commenced operations on 13 July 1985 using ex-London DMSs. By 1986 the first area scheme was implemented at Orpington, with Orpington Buses (a London Buses subsidiary) starting a twenty-five-bus operation from a base on an industrial estate in St Mary Cray using the fleetname Roundabout. As part of this scheme, route 51, one of Sidcup's trunk routes, was lost to London Country, who commenced operation on 16 June 1986 from a reopened Swanley garage using a mixture of indigenous AN class Atlanteans and second-hand versions from Southdown, Northern General and Strathclyde Transport. The full Orpington scheme came into effect on 15 August 1986, causing the closure of Bexleyheath garage, with its routes, vehicles and crews transferring to other garages – mainly Sidcup, Plumstead and New Cross. For the next two years things settled down: Bexleyheath garage was still used as the terminus for the 122 and 160, Sidcup and Plumstead ran most of the area's red bus network, and London Country carried on with its green bus routes. In the period covered in this book, London Country was split into four and privatised. Dartford and Swanley garages became part of London Country South East in September 1986. Other than removal of NBC symbols, little changed until April 1987 when the company became Kentish Bus, with a new maroon and cream livery, and a new fleet numbering system. Bexleyheath garage was used for storage, and for heats of the Bus Driver of the Year competition in 1987. Further area schemes followed in 1987 at Kingston and Harrow, based around London Buses' existing garages at Norbiton and Harrow Weald – in both cases using a mix of new minibuses, older single and new and old double-deck buses from various sources, including a batch of ex-West Midlands Volvo Ailsa buses and leased Mk II Metrobuses. Staff not only had to drive older buses, but would often face longer duties and worse pay, leading to inevitable unrest and industrial action.

The Bexley area routes were tendered in 1987, comprising massive reorganisation of the area's routes, with the former London Country routes becoming part of the network, and many other routes being adjusted, or brand-new routes introduced. In the early phases of tendering the routes had T1–4 route numbers for the 'big' bus routes and L1–5 route numbers for the minibus routes until the proper route numbers were finalised. These numbers appeared in some early publicity shots mainly taken at Eastbourne, who had borrowed four Ivecos for use on their 'Red Carpet' services and had received their blue and cream livery. One of their Fleetlines, 31, was painted into Bexleybus colours, while LS82 and DMS 2166 were also painted into Bexleybus colours, with the latter being fitted with route T5 blinds. Leyland's Olympian, E392 DHG, was also painted in Bexleybus livery, and fitted with Bexley area blinds.

London Buses' Selkent subsidiary won seventeen out of the twenty routes tendered, the remaining three routes being won by Boro'line Maidstone. The Selkent bid was won on the basis of reopening Bexleyheath garage as a separate low-cost operating unit within Selkent, but with the loss of the bulk of its routes, the recently rebuilt garage at Sidcup would close (Sidcup being too far from the network's centre).

The initial routes won by Selkent were the 96, 99, 178, 229, 244, 269, 272, 291, 401, 422, 469, 472, 492 and B11–15. Running these routes was to commence on 16 January 1988, with Sidcup garage closing the day before. The new operation was to be called Bexleybus, using buses in an attractive blue and cream livery, complete with their own numbering system starting at 1. The fleet comprised twenty-eight leased, single-door Olympians (a cancelled order and to full Manchester specifications). Twenty-four Leyland Nationals, surplus from within London Buses, were repainted by Eastbourne Buses, and twelve Ivecos with Robin Hood bodies came from Roundabout. Seventeen DMS Fleetlines came from the training fleet, or storage at AEC Southall, and were prepared and painted by Ensign. Finally, fourteen ex-Clydeside Scottish DMSs were prepared and painted by Clydeside in exchange for Routemasters. The DMSs had many differences between the two groups: Ensign's had two doors, working rear blind boxes and wider front blind boxes, while the Scottish ones had single doors, a painted-out rear blind box and smaller front blind boxes. Even the fleetname positions were different between the two groups, the Scottish ones being under the lower-deck windows and Ensign's being between decks. Meanwhile, Boro'line Maidstone set up a base for its routes (132, 228/328 and 233) at the

Crayford Depot of Bexley Council, and, pending the arrival of new vehicles, arranged to hire buses from various companies. Vehicles hired included Leyland Nationals from Eastbourne, Atlanteans from Hull and Manchester, and a handful of green Nationals from London Country North East.

Things did not go well for Bexleybus, however. There were staff shortages and breakdowns from the start, the garage did not have its full quota of drivers and buses that had been sitting idle in storage before refurbishment were increasingly unreliable. The tight headways and interworked routes just added to the problems, as buses delayed on one route would affect the next route it worked on. Bexleyheath garage had suffered from vandalism during its two-year closure, so portacabins were brought in for staff and admin facilities. The drivers faced an increasingly hostile public, leading to more drivers leaving, and industrial unrest added to the problems, which resulted in a rescheduling of the services on 14 May, but the problems continued. From November, routes 422 and 492 were reallocated to Boro'line to help Bexleybus match available resources to routes, but despite improvements to pay and the facilities at Bexleyheath, staff levels were never ideal.

Boro'line were not without problems either, and with the addition of routes 422 and 492 also started to suffer staff shortages, leading to an emergency timetable being implemented on both routes from 16 October. As the year progressed, Boro'line's new Olympians arrived for the Bexley routes, to be followed later in the year by Volvo Ailsas from Tayside and ex-London Leyland Nationals for the newly acquired routes 422 and 492. Boro'line also won route 188 (Greenwich to Euston) and commenced operation on 11 November 1988. This was also run from Crayford Depot using Ipswich Atlanteans and Nottingham Fleetlines, until the intended Volvo Citybuses arrived. Even after their arrival, various oddities from Crayford would escape for a day out in Central London.

Things had started to settle down by mid-1990 for Bexleybus: buses were being drafted in from other parts of the London Buses empire, including Titans, six of which got a repaint into Bexleybus blue and cream, taking Bexleybus numbers from the DMSs they replaced. However, many simply gained Bexleybus logos on their existing red livery when the decision was taken to cease using the attractive blue and cream colours. Moreover, all would now show their London Buses fleet numbers, the Bexleybus numbers also being dropped. The sole prototype Titan in the Selkent fleet, T1131, was allocated to Bexleyheath but transferred out before London Central took over.

When the area (except the block grant route B16) came up for retendering, the entire network was lost to other operators, principally London Central (99, 178, 229, 244, 291, 401, 469, B12 and B13) and Boro'line, (272 and 472), with Kentish Bus getting the trunk 96 route along with the 269 and B11. Transcity gained the B15, Boro'line kept the 132, 228/328, 233, 422 and 492, but did suffer one loss – the 188, which was won by Selkent, who allocated it to Plumstead garage. Meanwhile, London Central's tender had been based on a new depot being opened in nearby Belvedere, but had its planning application turned down. After negotiations, it was agreed that Selkent would transfer Bexleyheath garage to London Central for operating its newly won routes, along with the sole route kept by the garage, the B16. The garage was transferred to London Central on 24 November 1990, in advance of the new tenders commencing from 19 January 1991. Standard fleet numbers were applied to all buses, including the leased Olympians, which now showed numbers L264–71. All other classes received their original class codes and numbers.

As Boro'line were losing the 188 on 24 November 1990, but not taking up routes 272 and 472 until January 1991, LRT agreed to Boro'line assuming these routes on 24 November to avoid having to lay off (or lose) staff in the intervening weeks. The Bexleybus Olympians were stood down at the end of 1990 and returned to their lessors, appearing later in Blackburn, Hull, Liverpool, Manchester and Newcastle. The DMSs had all been withdrawn, but a few were pressed back into service at Merton, with their fronts having been repainted red. They appeared on most of the garages' routes in the few weeks before their final withdrawal, even appearing in their odd hybrid livery in Central London. The remaining fleet of Nationals, Metroriders, StarRiders and Ivecos were quickly repainted in standard London Central red. The handful of blue and cream Titans were also repainted back into red, despite them only just having been painted in Bexleybus colours!

Over at Boro'line, the loss of the 188 meant that the Volvos formerly used on that route now appeared on all the Bexleyheath and Woolwich routes, along with a handful of Ailsas, Ipswich Atlanteans, and the normal Lynxes and Olympians. However, all was not well at Boro'line, and with mounting losses, Maidstone Borough Council decided to sell the business. Maidstone & District, although interested, were not shortlisted as a potential buyer, and so registered competing routes in Maidstone. Boro'line quickly retaliated with competitive routes in Chatham, using a variety of buses from Maidstone. But now the end was near, and on 17 February 1992 the London operations were sold to Kentish Bus. Just two days later, Boro'line entered administration. All remaining Boro'line operations ceased on 29 May 1992. Kentish Bus quickly added its fleetnames to the ex-Boro'line London fleet, making the buses look even more down at heel, with some even running with odd panels in primer. A repaint program was quickly started, with buses then receiving standard Kentish Bus maroon and cream livery.

By the end of 1993, relative stability had been restored. Buses were once again red and run by the direct successors of London Transport, or London Country South East/Kentish Bus. Tendering continued, with routes being lost and gained, but never again on the scale of disruption of the initial Bexley Area Scheme. The scheme had many lasting effects; Bexleyheath garage is still open and still run by London Central, and the majority of the routes introduced on 16 January 1988 are still in use, with few changes. The massive Bluewater Shopping Centre saw many routes being extended from Dartford to the purpose-built bus station there, but the basic routes, such as 96 and 492, still travel the same routes from Dartford towards London. Sidcup garage was demolished for offices, but the admin block still survives. Dartford garage is now part of Arriva London and still runs many routes in South East London, including former Bexleybus route 229, which Bexleyheath lost in 2016 after many years at that garage. The 132 returned to

Bexleyheath garage via East Thames Buses in 2009, and both the 51 and 96 were won by Stagecoach London, both operating from Plumstead, and so it goes on. Without doubt more changes will occur, but with TfL's rigid controls it's unlikely anything as fast-paced and colourful will happen to the area's bus network again!

This book is not meant as an exhaustive history of Bexley's buses or routes, but as an overview showing the variety of colours and vehicles used over a ten-year period, which ultimately settled into a long-lasting network. Excellent sources used in the writing of this book are LOTS (*London Bus Magazine* vol. 99, out of print, is devoted to Bexleybus) and the websites countrybus.org and londonbusroutes.net, both of which are very useful. All pictures are my own, unless credited. If I have missed or wrongly credited a picture, please accept my apologies. We will make the necessary corrections at the first available opportunity.

Waiting time at Bexleyheath garage (BX) in June 1983 is MD93. It was based at the new Plumstead garage (PD), which opened in 1981, replacing the old Plumstead and Abbey Wood garages. MD93 would be sold to Reading Transport later that year.

On the same day, DMS 2404 is seen opposite Bexleyheath garage, awaiting a new driver to work on the 89. New to BX, it was transferred away later that year, and would last until 1991 before scrapping.

Seen at the old bus station at Eltham Well Hall in March 1983, DMS 2399 will soon leave on the circular 132. The 132 would cease to be a circular under the Bexleybus scheme, running instead from Bexleyheath to Eltham via Bexley.

Three of Sidcup's (SP) Titans are seen slumbering in this October 1987 picture. T770, nearest the camera, would finish its service life with Stagecoach East Kent.

While working the 269 to Sidcup, Queen Mary's Hospital, DMS 2509 has a spot of trouble, and the duty inspectors prepare to transfer the passengers. DMS 2509 would spend the last two years of London service as a training bus.

Passengers disembark from DMS 2509 to continue their journey on a replacement bus. Under Bexleybus the 269 will be converted to single-deck and extended to Bromley, but will lose its Bexleyheath–Woolwich section to new route 469.

On April 10 1983, sixteen DMSs slumber inside Bexleyheath garage. On the right an unidentified Titan heralds the end of the DMSs at this garage.

Bexleyheath operated both standard and B20 type DMSs. Seen in 1983, DMS 2347 stands on the garage forecourt beside DMS 860, which would be scrapped in 1984. DMS 2347 became a training bus in 1992, before withdrawal in 1994.

Awaiting a new driver, DMS 2365 sits outside its home garage. The 89 was left unaltered by Bexleybus (the route transferring to New Cross (NX)) and still runs from Lewisham to Slade Green. It is seen in March 1983.

The small MD class bowed out in 1983, complete with a farewell tour from PD over its old routes. Here, MD127 makes a photo stop on Bostall Heath. After appearing in a special white 'For Sale' livery at the Aldenham Spectacular, it would be sold to Leicester.

Sidcup still had an allocation of RMs in 1983, and on 14 June RM501 is seen leaving Foots Cray on the long journey to Moorgate. The 21 would convert to one-man operated (OPO) in February 1988, while RM501 was later sold to Clydeside Scottish.

DMS 2413 is seen leaving Bexleyheath Clock Tower. Converted to a driver training bus in 1992, it would perform this duty for a further three years. The area behind the bus has totally changed, with a new road cutting across this area and a small bus stand roughly where the trees are.

On 14 June, M805 is seen joining route 229, heading from Sidcup garage to Green Street Green. M805 was one of a small group of Metrobuses allocated to Sidcup for comparative trials between Metrobuses, DMSs and Titans.

Another of the trials buses, M802 is seen on the 51, awaiting a new driver to walk up from Sidcup garage using the path beside the houses on the right. M802 was scrapped in December 2008.

On 15 March 1983, DMS 2522 is seen at the Market Street, Dartford, terminus of the 96. DMS 2522 would work at various South London garages before withdrawal in 1991. The 96 has kept to the same route since its introduction in 1959, replacing trolleybus route 696. Its extension to the Bluewater shopping complex came in 1999.

DMS 2380 stands at the head of four B20 DMSs beside Bexleyheath garage, having been replaced by Titans. DMS 2380 was moved to Croydon, Thornton Heath and Stockwell, before becoming a training vehicle at Plumstead.

The new order: T763 is seen at Dartford on 17 June, when two months old. A side blind has been used as the ultimate destination. Later in life, T763 would be converted to open-top and exported to the USA.

Titan T730 is only a month old when seen outside Bexleyheath garage on the 269 to Woolwich in April 1983. Later being sold to Merseybus, T730 ended up with Stagecoach and then Blue Triangle before being exported to Italy.

To keep the training of drivers on L class Olympians moving smoothly, new Olympians were delivered to Bexleyheath. L65, seen in June 1983 at the side of the garage, was to spend all its life in South London, ending up with the Metropolitan Police for training purposes.

Speeding past its home garage, L45 heads towards Bromley. Privatised into the Cowie South London fleet (which became Arriva South London), it stayed in London until its sale to Ensign Bus in 2005.

T64 and L50 stand in front of Bexleyheath garage. Plumstead-allocated T64 would transfer back to East London, finally being withdrawn in November 1994, while L50 would leave London in 2005, being sold to Ensign Bus.

T745 stands beside a pile of destination blinds on the last night at Bexleyheath. As the buses came in, the blinds were removed and the buses were driven out to their new homes, with most going to Sidcup and Plumstead.

Leaving BX for its new home at Sidcup, the driver of T721 receives instructions before departure. Withdrawn from London service in 2001, it passed via Ensign to Rennies, Dunfermline, lasting until final withdrawal in 2008.

On the last night at Bexleyheath, a crowd of staff, well-wishers and enthusiasts waited for the last bus in – T799 on the 269, driven by Bob Baker. T799 had also been Bexleyheath's only all-over advert-liveried bus, which publicised the local shopping centre.

On the next day (16 August 1986), London Country took over the 51 from Sidcup using existing and second-hand Atlanteans, such as AN327, which came from Glasgow. To serve the route, the old London Country garage at Swanley was reopened.

The day after – Bexleyheath garage, as seen on 17 August 1983, with buses serving the 160 and 122 on the stand, looking rather lost! The 160 would cease to serve Bexleyheath in August 1989 when new route B16 was introduced while the 122 would be replaced on the Plumstead to Bexleyheath section by Bexleybus 422.

After spending a couple of years in a special white/red livery for express route 177E from Plumstead, T112 and T113 are seen having just been repainted back into standard fleet red. As luck would have it, both were sitting on the stand at Bexleyheath, on the 122 to Crystal Palace, when seen.

Seen at Bexleyheath Clock Tower on 28 June 1988 is L40, which is returning on the 229 to its home garage. The Autocheck posters refer to an experimental ticketing scheme run in Bexley area, with buses at BX, PD and SP suitably equipped. As with many of these schemes, however, it was not a success.

Standing at the new Eltham bus station on 7 June 1987 is Sidcup's L34, which will be making its way clockwise around the 132 loop from Eltham to Crook Log, Bexleyheath and Bexley, and then back to Eltham. A yellow ultimate blind indicated travelling the loop anticlockwise.

On the stand in Bexleyheath in June 1987 is T738, which is awaiting another working on the 229. After London service, T738 went to work for Stagecoach Devon, before finishing its days with Stagecoach North West.

Olympians L41 (SP) and L29 (PD) stand at Bexleyheath in June 1987. Route 269A, running between Woolwich (Charlton at peaks) and Bexleyheath, lasted just four years from 1984, until it was replaced in part by the new Bexleybus route 401.

When Hanwell's 207 was converted to one-person operation, the RMLs were briefly stored at Bexleyheath. RML2499 is seen inside the garage, with its engine running, on 29 March 1987. In 2002, it was one of a number of buses to receive a gold vinyl wrap for the Queen's Jubilee, reverting to red at the year's end.

Seen through a smoke-filled garage on the same day is former Hanwell RML2474, which lasted in London passenger service until 2004. It was bought by the Moseleys Museum, Pontefract.

North Street's T90 is seen leaving Bexleyheath, where heats of the Bus Driver of the Year had been taking place. T90 finished its London career working for London & Country on the 188.

Also seen on 26 June 1987 leaving Bexleyheath is Plumstead garage's Selkent Travel-liveried L263, one of four coach-seated Olympians delivered to Selkent. L263 was the last bus bodied by ECW and is now preserved at the East Anglia Transport Museum.

A type not seen at Bexleyheath was the Leyland National. Here, Leyton's LS101 leaves the garage. Leyland Nationals would return in the Bexleybus era, and LS101 would return to spend three months at BX from November 1990.

A type never allocated to Bexleyheath was the Metrobus. Here, Edgware's M289 makes its way back to its home shed. During privatisation, M289 became part of London General, who sold it in 2000 to Ensign Bus.

A view of London Country's Dartford garage on 15 March 1983, with SNB151 resting outside the garage buildings in between duties on the 400. This garage would be replaced by larger, more modern facilities nearby.

Kentish Bus 645, an ex-Glasgow Atlantean, is caught in Mayplace Road, Bexleyheath, on the 486 to Thamesmead, which will be part replaced by the 401 under Bexleybus. Although 645 is still in London Country South East livery, the fleet number gives away its real owner.

Working route 492, Kentish Bus 467 is seen outside Bexleyheath garage. This bus would be converted to a National Greenway in 1992 and be re-registered SIB 1283, returning to service at Dunton Green on route 227. It would end up with Blackburn Transport after a spell with Arriva in Teesside.

Seen in Bexleyheath in July 1987 while working the 400 to Dartford is Kentish Bus Leyland National 456. Route 400 would later become part of Bexleybus' route 422, running from Woolwich to Bexleyheath, while Leyland National 456 would be transferred to parent company Northumbria.

Still bearing the NBC symbol and London Country lettering on its upper panels, Kentish Bus 431 is seen loading on the 492 in a now pedestrianised part of Bexleyheath Broadway in mid-March 1987. Its repaint into Kentish Bus colours came in 1988, followed a year later by its transfer to Northumbria.

Seen in Mayplace Road, Bexleyheath, Kentish Bus 450 heads to Thamesmead on the 486 in July 1987, still looking like a London Country bus; a repaint into Kentish Bus maroon and cream would come later, in 1988. Route 486 would also become part of Bexleybus route 422.

Passing through part of Bexleyheath, which has changed greatly, Kentish Bus 483 makes its way to South Darenth. The route was curtailed at Dartford with the coming of Bexleybus, before later being extended to Bluewater Shopping Centre.

Tucked into a corner of Sidcup garage in May 1987 is preserved RM8 and BEL's RMA6. RM8 was used as the Chiswick test bus until being allocated to Sidcup in 1976, where it was adopted as the garage showbus and was cared for by the RM8 Group. Painted into 1933 London Transport livery in 1983, it would be repainted red in 1984. BEL would sell RMA6 into preservation later in 1983.

In the same corner, but seen in October 1987, are RM8, T737 and T740. Route 286 was a somewhat quiet local route, which became minibus operated in 1989. Extended to Sidcup, Queen Mary's Hospital, in 2000, a return to full-size single-deck buses was very much welcome.

Descending Sidcup Hill, M803 is seen on the 228. This route was replaced by 228A and 228C in November 1986, which in turn were replaced by the 228 and 328 under the Bexleybus scheme, operated by Boro'line. M803 stayed with Arriva South London until withdrawn in 2001.

Roadworks closed Sidcup High Street in March 1983, and diverted buses used roads they did not normally traverse. Here, RM417 rejoins the route on its way back to its depot. Sidcup was RM417's last garage, being withdrawn there in 1985.

Seen in Foots Cray on 16 June 1983 is M803. The 51 has had many operators, garages and types of bus in the last thirty years, but the route itself has seen virtually no change.

Local route 21A had been gradually shortened over the years, having lost the Sidcup–Eltham section in 1982. Now just running between Swanley and Sidcup, it would be replaced with route 233 in October 1984. M800 is seen on 16 June 1983.

RM2200 has just left Sidcup garage to take up service on the 161. The 161 would be cut back to serve Sidcup in the peak hours only, before losing its allocation to Plumstead and then finally ceasing to serve Sidcup altogether.

Olympians and Titans at rest in SP on 30 June 1987. T854, nearest, worked for Stagecoach West & Wales before being broken up for spares by Stagecoach West Scotland.

Sometimes buses turning at Sidcup garage would spill out onto the street, as seen with T802 and T1086 on a murky January morning in 1988. T1086 was another Titan to see further service in Merseyside.

Fire destroyed four Titans at SP on 7 December 1987. Here are the remains of T734 and T758 shortly after the fire. (M. J. Beckham)

Here are the sad remains of T900 and T708. Following the fire, T900 was only four years old when destroyed. (M. J. Beckham)

Sidcup's last day was 15 January 1988, and to mark the occasion RT1702 toured some of the garage's routes. It is seen here by the administration block, which still stands to this day. As well as blinds for the 21A, it also carries a slip board commemorating the garage's closure.

While the Roundabout Ivecos were being repainted into Bexleybus livery, some Bexleybus Metroriders were lent to Roundabout. One of them, 34, is seen on the R11 at Foots Cray, overtaking a Kentish Bus Atlantean on the 51. (T. Burnham)

Also used by Roundabout was Bexleybus 30, which is similarly seen on the R11. Note the London Regional Transport (LRT) service logo on the front, a position not used in Bexleybus days. (T. Burnham)

Eastbourne Buses were involved in the repainting of buses, storage, and inspection of new buses for Bexleybus. Olympian 1 (E901 KYR) is seen undergoing inspection at Eastbourne Buses' Birch Road Depot in 1987. (A. Cornell)

Another view of Olympian 1 while in Eastbourne. After Bexleybus, this bus saw service with Sunderland Busways, Stagecoach Hull and Judds before its final withdrawal and preservation in 2014. (A. Cornell)

Bexleybus Iveco 73 (D520 FYL *Teal*) attended the Gravesend Bus Rally in 1987. It is seen displaying route number L4, which would become the B14 when it was decided to have the minibus routes in the B series. Note the large Bexleybus fleetname and lack of Hoppa branding.

Parked at a foggy Plumstead garage on 15 January 1988 is THM 657M. Although showing its Bexleybus, LRT and Autocheck signage, no fleet number (82) has been applied under the driver's side window.

On 15 January 1987, the penultimate day before closure, Metrorider 37 is parked outside Sidcup's administration block, minus its Bexleybus logos.

Parked in front of 37 at Sidcup is Iveco 72 (C518 DYM *Sandpiper*), which is also missing its Bexleybus name. After London service, it would be bought by Viscount, Peterborough.

A look into Bexleyheath on 17 April 1988 reveals an impressive line-up of fifteen DMSs, a handful of Leyland Nationals and an Olympian poking its front into the picture.

Two DMSs are seen at Geddes Place, Bexleyheath stand, showing the differences between the buses refurbished by Ensign and the batch refurbished by Clydeside; namely, the fleetname position, blind box, indicators and being single door (Scotland) and dual door (Ensign).

Bexleybus 90 is seen on route 401 on a short working to Belvedere in August 1987. At this time the 401 was running to Woolwich, but was later cut back to Thamesmead and Dartford Heath on school days. The Dartford Heath service was later replaced by school route 601.

Making a right turn in Bexleyheath is Bexleybus 100, which is seen working the 96. When new this bus was fitted with experimental seating moquette – later used in both Titans and Metrobuses. This DMS lasted until 1990, with storage and scrapping taking place in the same year.

Showing its two-door format, Bexleybus 96 was one of the DMSs that later had its front painted red. It worked various services from Merton and Fulwell before its sale to Big Bus Co. and later export to the USA.

Former Scottish DMS 82 loads while working the 469. The 469 was a direct replacement for the 269A and part of the 229, and under the original proposals it would have been route T3. 82 was withdrawn in January 1989.

Bexleybus 85 heads for Foots Cray on the 229 on 2 May 1989. Later, the 229 would be diverted to terminate at Sidcup, Queen Marys Hospital, where it still turns thirty years later. 85 was withdrawn in August 1989.

A rear view of 77 – not only the oldest DMS in the Bexleybus fleet (new in 1973), but the only one to retain its rear engine shrouds. Seen parked at BX on 28 June 1989, it was withdrawn three months later.

Standing on the forecourt of BX in April 1988 is Bexleybus 89. New in 1974, it was allocated to London sightseeing duties before settling down to more mundane work. Seen when fourteen years old, it would be stored in August 1989, with scrapping soon following.

The newest of the DMSs, 107 was used for early PR shots while stored at Eastbourne Buses, using just its number '2166' and carrying blinds for the proposed T-numbered routes in 1987. 107 would be withdrawn and scrapped in 1990.

Lewisham bus station is the setting for Bexleybus 81 and Metrobus DMS 1977. The Metrobus DMS would go on to sightseeing work in the USA, whereas 81 would be scrapped in 1990.

Route 422 would be reallocated to Boro'line Maidstone in November 1988 to help Bexleybus better match resources to its schedule requirements. Bexleybus 43 basks in the sun in May 1988. Sold to Provincial in 1991, 43 (LS28) would carry on in service until the end of 1997.

Arriving in Bexleyheath, 59 makes for Bromley on the 269. Seen in February 1988, 59 would be stored, then scrapped in 1991. The 269 is still running between Bexleyheath and Bromley.

Leyland National 53, also on the 269, picks up passengers at Bexleyheath garage. With the loss of the 422 and 492, LS178 became surplus. It was stored at various locations before being sold for scrap in 1990.

National 60 is parked outside Plumstead garage in this April 1988 picture. Another bus deemed surplus at the end of 1988, it would be withdrawn and scrapped by 1991.

This June 1990 view of 43 shows it looking a little more careworn than our earlier view; however, it still had a few months left before its withdrawal and sale to Provincial, with whom it worked until final withdrawal came around 1998.

Route 244 was one of Bexleybus' shorter routes, running between Woolwich, where LS428 is seen, and Broadwaters. LS428 was now nearing the end of the road, withdrawal coming in 1991. (A. J. Smith)

Route 492 was also lost to Boro'line in November 1988. In this February 1988 view, 48 heads through Bexleyheath for Sidcup station beneath a stormy sky. Bexleybus 48 (LS120) survived with independents until around 2000.

Seen changing drivers near Bexleyheath, LS50 (Bexleybus 45) is working the 96 to Woolwich. It would be sold off for scrap in 1991. (A. J. Smith)

On the 492 in Dartford, National 57 loads for Sidcup station. With the loss of the 492 in November 1988, 57 became surplus to requirements and was sold to Fountain Coaches, then moving to Westbus before being scrapped in 1993. (A. J. Smith)

Olympian 12 shows its rear aspect. Like many of the class, 12 went to Busways, Newcastle, then Hull (Stagecoach) before sale to Wealden PSV. Being single-doored slowed down loading and unloading, making them unpopular with staff and passengers.

Bexleybus 16 is caught leaving BX to take up service on the 272. 16 went onto further service in Liverpool, working for Fareway, Merrseybus, Arriva and Aintree Coachlines.

In this June 1988 view, 15 loads for Woolwich on the 469. December 1990 would see 15 returned off lease and follow its sisters to Newcastle and Hull.

Coach-seated Olympian 3 and Iveco 76 are seen at the Gravesend Riverside Bus Rally in July 1989. Note the Bexleybus recruitment advert on the Iveco. Olympian 3 was exported to Singapore in 1992, while 76 was sold to Midland Fox.

A grey day in Dartford finds 24, now showing its L number under the windscreen. L287 followed the well-trodden path to Newcastle and Hull before scrapping in 2008. This had been the 96's stand for many years, until the massive shopping complex at Bluewater opened, with the 96 being extended there with non-stop running from Dartford. (A. J. Smith)

Seen outside Bexleyheath garage, 13 overtakes 91 on the 229, which has just changed drivers, in June 1988. Despite its smart appearance, 91 went for scrap in 1990.

On the stand at Geddes Place, Bexleyheath, is 26 (L289). After Bexleybus it went to work in Merseyside, before a conversion to part open-top, and sale to PD Travel, Glasgow. It is believed that 26 was scrapped in 2008.

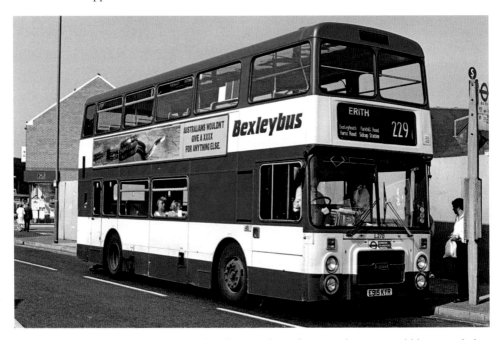

Now renumbered L278, Bexleybus 15 heads to Erith on the 229. The 229 would be extended to Thamesmead in 1994, which is still its current terminus today (2018). L278 finished its service life with TM Travel in 2008.

Making a sharp left turn on the 401 on 21 July 1990 is L273. L273 had a long life, working in Sunderland, Hull, Blackburn and finally with Powell, Hellaby. Originally running to Woolwich, the 401 was cut back to terminate at Thamesmead in 1991.

Coach-seated Olympian 3 is seen in High Holborn on 11 August 1988 while on a private hire. Bexleybus 3 was exported to Singapore in 1992, along with the other two coach-seated Olympians, 2 and 4.

Showing plain 268 as its number, the former 5 (E905 KYR) is on the 99 to Erith. Route 99 ran between Woolwich and Erith, with buses interworking this route with the 272. 5 went to Sunderland, Hull, Preston and Kent. The scrapman called around 2014. (A. J. Smith)

Olympian 6 (L269) waits time in Woolwich on the 472 Shoppers Express, which was a short-lived route, starting in February 1988 and being replaced by the X72 in 1994. In its short life, it was run by Bexleybus, Boro'line and Kentish Bus.

27 (E927 KYR) is seen parked up at BX. Following the same path around the north of England, 27 ended its passenger-carrying days back in the south, with Shamrock, Poole.

Another short-lived service was the 480X, linking Oxford Circus and Gravesend on three consecutive Saturdays in January 1990. On 20 January, Bexleybus 26 takes a short break before returning to Gravesend.

26 (E926 KYR) is seen leaving Oxford Circus on the long run to Gravesend. 26 was to run in Liverpool, Leicester and Dunstable, before conversion to part open-top. It would be scrapped in 2009.

By March 1989, having had routes 422 and 492 reassigned, Bexleybus were able to undertake private hires and rail replacement work. On 5 March, Olympian 7 is seen at Dartford station, awaiting a driver. (A. J. Smith)

Route 272 linked Woolwich and Thamesmead. Here, Olympian 18 is seen loading in Woolwich for Thamesmead. The route lasted until 1999, when it was withdrawn, with both the 472 and 244 covering its route. (A. J. Smith)

The B12 linked Erith and Bexleyheath via Bexleyheath station. Iveco 65 was new to Orpington Buses, as RH11, where it carried the name *Sparrow*. Sold in 1991, 65 ended its career on Tyneside.

Iveco 68, now carrying its original number, RH14, is seen in Bexleyheath on 22 August 1990 with a slight livery variation; namely, the blue extends up to the roof. When new at Roundabout, it carried the name *Nightingale*.

New as RH12 *Woodpecker* to Roundabout, 66 was repainted by Eastbourne Buses into Bexleybus colours. After Bexleybus, 65 was to see service with Viscount in Peterborough. It is seen here minus its Bexley Hoppa branding on the B12 in May 1989.

Metrorider 29 is seen in February 1988, taking up service on the B11 to Lodge Hill. Upon reassignment to Kentish Bus in 1991, the route was extended to Abbey Wood.

Route B13 started out as short route between Bexleyheath and Halfway Street (between Blackfen and New Eltham), but in November 1988 it was extended over the withdrawn B14 to Erith. In 1991 a further extension stretched the route from Halfway Street to the better traffic objective at New Eltham station. Here, MR55 sets off with a good load for Erith in July 1990.

Displaying the B13 Halfway Street destination, Metrorider 30 waits time at Bexleyheath, in July 1990. Repainted red in 1991, MR54 worked for Rhondda Bus before returning to the South East with Thorpes.

Metrorider 39 was a Bexleybus blue bus until it was repainted red in 1991. After London, 39 had spells in Uttoxeter and Cardiff.

Route B14 lasted from January 1988 until November 1988, when it was replaced by an extension of the B13, as mentioned previously. Many years later the number 'B14' would be used for a Bexleyheath to Sidcup and Orpington minibus route. Bexleybus 31 arrives from Erith in February 1988.

The B15 started life running between Welling and Joydens Wood, with different routings depending on the time of day. This continued even after Transcity took over in 1991. Metrorider 34 is seen parked at BX.

In July 1989, new route B16 replaced the 160 between Eltham and Welling, and the B1 on to Kidbrooke. Six Mercedes StarRiders in full Bexleybus livery were allocated to the route, as shown by 110, which is seen in July 1989.

StarRider 110 shows its rear aspect at BX in August 1989. It would be repainted red in June the following year, staying in London until its sale to MK Metro, Milton Keynes, in 2000.

Leaving Bexleyheath on driver training duties is Iveco G135 GOL, which was used for training and crew ferry work.

Coach LD4 was obtained for private hire work, but was also used on various routes, including the 96 and 229 during October and November 1989. It is seen parked at Bezleyheath on 5 February 1989.

Six Titans joined Bexleybus, taking the fleet numbers of the DMSs they replaced. One of them, 89 (T764), rests at Bexleyheath. 89 was painted blue in August 1989 but was quickly repainted red in May 1990.

It is Boxing Day 1989, and Titans 84 and 104 sit between 25 and 46. Bexleybus did not operate services on this day. Titan 104 lasted nine months in blue; meanwhile, 84 would be withdrawn by London Central in 1997, and is currently preserved in Bexleybus colours.

A wider view of Bexleyheath on Boxing Day 1989, showing solid blue and the Bexleybus name looking proudly over the garage. On this day Kentish Bus operated a limited service on the 96 and 272 on behalf of LRT.

Another view of T952 parked at Geddes Place, Bexleyheath. It lasted in Bexleybus livery for sixteen months – longer than most of the six blue Titans. Sold to Ensign in 2001, it was bought by GTL, Liverpool, before finally being broken up around 2003.

It is July 1990, and Bexleybus blue is under attack. Between the Olympians is the former Bexleybus 35, while SR57 has become red after eleven months in blue.

It is November 1990. The Bexleybus sign survives and the transferred-in Titans and long Metrorider have Bexleybus fleetnames, but the blue livery is now becoming rare. Metrorider MRL66 was new to Roundabout, leaving London after a mere seven years of service.

MR31, a former Harrow Buses Metrorider, was used by Bexleyheath in early 1990 under the number 41 (previously used on Bexleybus National LS18), which was hand-written above front nearside wheel. (M. J. Beckham)

Although proudly proclaiming Selkent, Bexleyheath will soon become a London Central garage. The Olympian L286 would go off lease and Metrorider MR55 would turn red.

To mark the end of the Bexleybus/Selkent era, RM2046 made a number of trips over the Bexleybus routes. It is seen here blinded and ready for the 269 to Bromley North. (M. J. Beckham).

The Olympians would return to their lessor; here, 20 (L283) stands at the head of a line of out-of-service Olympians on 27 January 1991.

London Central buses, and no blue: T888 stands under the new London Central sign, gleaming in its fresh coat of red paint.

After Selkent's new Titans and Olympians that previously worked on the 51, Kentish Bus offered older Atlanteans. Seen here is an N-registered ex-Southdown example. More modern stock would follow in later years. Note the smartly uniformed driver. (T. Burnham)

While awaiting new vehicles, Boro'line hired in buses from far and wide. Seen at Eltham is Scania N113 demonstrator E26 ECH. Possibly being used as a crew ferry bus, it is nonetheless ready for LRT work, complete with destination blind. (M. J. Beckham)

Also found in Eltham was Maidstone & District Metrobus 5207. Without LRT service boards, but blinded for the 233, it is complete with an ultimate destination blind. Note the new Olympian hiding behind it. (M. J. Beckham)

GM Buses-livered LJA 631P was used, complete with adverts for Manchester's Little Gem minibuses and GM Buses fleetnames alongside Boro'line ones. Seen in February 1988 on the 132, it would return north in May.

From Kingston upon Hull came Atlanteans. On 23 January 1988, 376 is caught in Eltham bus station with Boro'line fleetnames, fully blinded for the 132.

Another KHCT vehicle, 375 is seen on the same day on the 233 to Swanley. The last of the KHCT buses would depart the fleet in in May.

An older Hull Atlantean hired was 343, one of their M-registered examples. Although no destination is shown, it is on the Eltham–Sidcup–Eltham circular, route 328. This bus had its top deck destroyed after a collision with a digger on Sidcup Hill in February, fortunately with the three upper-deck passengers only suffering minor injuries. The bus was not repaired, and was soon scrapped.

KHCT 382 was also used; it is seen here in February 1988, leaving Bexleyheath for Eltham on the 132.

When Boro'line won the 188 in November 1988, more buses were hired from Ipswich and Nottingham. Seen lined up in Bexley Council's Crayford Depot are buses from both fleets, with large LRT service logos hiding the Nottingham City Transport name beneath. Some of the Ipswich Atlanteans had their fleetnames over the cab/front door similarly treated.

By April, Boro'line's new vehicles were arriving – including this former Volvo B10M Citybus demonstrator, E164 OMD. With a Scottish-style destination box, 764 loads for Eltham on the 132.

New vehicles also included two Scania N112DRs, both of which were delivered in all-over white. Here, 702 is seen in July 1989, loading at Bexleyheath on the 132. Both Scanias would receive all-over advertising on the white base for Crayford Motors.

Sister 701 looks scruffy on the 132, complete with two sets of blinds in two different colours! Neither Scania would receive Maidstone fleet colours.

Buses from the Maidstone fleet also helped Crayford out. In May 1989, Bedford 272 is seen fully blinded for the 422.

When the new Olympians were delivered, temporary blinds were fitted – note the spelling of Bexleyheath. 755 glistens on the stand at Eltham, alongside London Buses LS216.

A small batch of Tayside Volvo Ailsas were purchased. Here, 915 swings into the corner while working the 492 in May 1989.

Former London Buses Leyland Nationals were also brought into the fleet. Boro'line 904 was formerly London Buses LS436, which was acquired from Ensign Bus. Seen in February 1989, it would be scrapped just two years later.

Another of Maidstone's Bedfords, 276 is seen on the 422, terminating at Bexleyheath, in May 1989.

As deliveries of Volvos for the 188 progressed, Ipswich Atlanteans became more common on the Bexley routes. Here, 85 is seen on the 422, with plenty of route information for the 188 and loads of LRT bus signs, but only a paper number in the windscreen for the 422.

Looking as if it were in Ipswich, 4 starts out on the 422 in Bexleyheath – the piece of paper in the windscreen tells us it really is on LRT route 422.

Now equipped with the correct blinds, 754 and 761 stand at Bexleyheath. Although showing full 228 blinds, 754 was on crew ferry duties when seen on 29 August 1989. Olympian 753 is preserved in Boro'line colours.

This time out for a spin on the 492, Bedford 276 swings left at Geddes Place, Bexleyheath, in May 1989.

Ipswich 94, showing both Ipswich and Boro'line fleetnames, arrives in Bexleyheath on the 422. The blinds have already been changed for the return journey – no pieces of paper here!

Showing some of Boro'line's varied fleet in this June 1990 view are Ipswich 94 (with full blinds), Olympian 760 (on the 132) and Ipswich 84 (without blinds). Hiding at the back is a Bexleybus-branded red Titan.

Olympian 754 is seen in the August 1990 sunshine, setting off for Dartford on the 492. 754 joined Kentish Bus, then Arriva Kent Thameside, before finally being withdrawn in 2002.

Ipswich 86 and 94 are seen at Bexleyheath in June 1990. Both now display full blind displays, in this case for the 422, but 86 still carries route branding for the 188.

Another ex-London National was 903 (London LS380), which also came to Boro'line via Ensign Bus in 1988. It would be withdrawn in 1991. Note the second-hand blind that was fitted when the bus was acquired.

Any type of vehicle could be found on the 422. In June 1990, an immaculate and fully blinded ex-Tayside Ailsa 915 takes a turn. Note that the Astor bingo hall has been demolished behind the bus.

One of a batch of twelve Lynx new to Boro'line for the 108, 808 is seen on the 492 in March 1991. After service with Kentish Bus, and later Arriva Kent Thameside as its 3061, it would be transferred to Arriva Cymru in late 1999.

Boro'line also took a batch of six Leyland Olympians upon the successful retendering of the 132, this time with Northern Counties bodies. As usual, they were pressed into service without a destination blind. 765 gleams at Bexleyheath in March 1991. One of this batch, 769, is preserved.

On 22 December 1990, Boro'line's heritage PD2A, 26, made an appearance on the 422, complete with Santa at the wheel. Route information was provided by a hand-written notice in the blind box. Here it stands at Geddes Place in failing light. (M. J. Beckham)

Centrewest-branded LS218 stands beside Bexleybus LS28. After three years at Bexleybus, LS28 was sold to People's Provincial, lasting there until the end of 1997. LS218 left London in 1992 and then worked with Shamrock, Pontypridd, until 1998.

The 89 had been reallocated to New Cross garage when Bexleybus commenced and received a small extension from Lewisham to New Cross Gate for garage journeys. Titan T875 is seen passing Bexleyheath garage in July 1990.

After withdrawal from Bexleyheath in 1990, four of the Bexleybus DMSs were briefly used at Merton, with their fronts repainted red, grey skirt, London Buses roundels and DMS numbers added. On 15 March, DMS 2143 is seen showing an incorrect destination as it leaves Euston on the 77.

More Titans arrived for DMS replacement in 1990. In July 1990, T753 heads out on the 229, complete with Bexleybus fleetnames and London Buses roundels. After London, T753 saw service on Merseyside before returning south to Nu-Venture, Aylesford.

New as Roundabout RH15 *Kingfisher*, this bus donned Bexleybus colours as Bexleybus 69 before a repaint into red, complete with Bexleybus logos. After Bexleybus, and another spell at Orpington, it was sold to Luton & District.

Seen at Bexleyheath Clock Tower, T1034 heads for Dartford as another Titan overtakes it. In later years, T1034 was transferred from Stagecoach Selkent to Stagecoach United Counties, before its eventual sale to Ensign Bus.

Roundabout RH8 *Swan* was transferred to Bexleyheath for two months from August 1990. As a loan bus, it wasn't fitted with a number blind with a 'B' on it, so it could only show numbers; in this instance, it is working the B15. Note the Selkent bag on the driver's shoulder, showing all the Selkent group fleetnames, including Bexleybus.

MR56 (Bexleybus 32) is shown on 28 May 1990, just after it has been repainted into red, but before the application of roundels, etc. New in December 1987, it would be withdrawn from London in 1993, moving to Cardiff.

New to Roundabout as RH18 *Sandpiper*, this bus then became Bexleybus 72. In this June 1990 view, it has just been repainted into red but still awaits its roundels, etc. Withdrawn in early 1991, RH18 was sold to Viscount, Peterborough.

New in 1983, T791 was transferred into Bexleyheath, quickly gaining Bexleybus logos, only to be transferred out a year later to Plumstead. Under Stagecoach Selkent, it would be transferred to Stagecoach Fife, in 1997.

T747 was delivered in gold as T1983 (in 1983) to celebrate the LT Jubilee. It would arrive at Bexleyheath in November 1990, staying there until withdrawal in 1997. Bought by Sullivan Buses and repainted in its gold livery, it was sold on to Talisman in 2012.

Painted in full London Central red livery, MR57 is caught on the B12 in March 1991. Route B12 was interlinked with the B11, but joint operation ceased in November 1988 for the benefit of both routes.

Optare MRL137 was new to Bexleyheath for the B16, and went into service in London Central red livery. Seen in January 1991, it had a short service life in London, being sold in 1999.

London Central had a small fleet of Mercedes minibuses, which seemed to spend their time going from garage to garage. MTL5, seen here blinded for the B16, spent a short time at Bexleyheath.

Green Line route 726 was still an orbital route, running from Dartford to Windsor via Croydon and Heathrow. It ran through the Bexleybus area but was not an LRT route until 1991. Kentish Bus 108 leaves Bexleyheath in July 1990 on its way to Croydon.

The 726 would lose its Heathrow–Windsor section and joined the LRT network in 1991, with the two existing operators, Kentish Bus and London Country North West, running it on a six-month temporary contract. Kentish Bus Leyland National 477 is seen at West Croydon while on its way to Heathrow – all a far cry from its Greenline heyday.

When the temporary contract finished, the route was awarded to London Coaches, with new DAF buses being allocated to London Coaches' Northfleet base. DK10 is seen loading at West Croydon in March 1992, just after London Coaches took over the route.

One of the more unusual Titans transferred to BX by Selkent was prototype T1131. Bought from Fishwicks, Leyland, it would leave BX in November 1990, going into store, then into service at Bromley. After seeing service at various other companies, it went into preservation in 1997. Seen here at BX along with RM2046, which was fundraising for 1990s Telethon.

Transcity of Sidcup's Peugeot-Talbot Pullman G147TGX rests between trips on the 492A, which Transcity ran commercially and was not part of the LRT network. These buses would work the B15 from January 1991 and would become part of the Kentish Bus fleet upon takeover in 1993.

In June 2018, Arriva London T316 heads along Station Road, Sidcup, on the 229. At the time of writing the route still links Sidcup and Thamesmead, but the bus is based at the former Kentish Bus garage at Dartford, which is still coded DT. Arriva is the direct descendant of Kentish Bus, but is now owned by the German company DB, as noted under the main fleetname.

Seen on the same day is Stagecoach 15069. After the early days of tendering, when elderly ex-Scottish Atlanteans could be found on the 51, modern low-floor Scanias are the norm, mixed in with other diesel and hybrid buses from Stagecoach's Plumstead garage. The garage, which opened in 1981, also provides buses for former Bexleybus routes 96, 291, 422 and 472.